CARYL CHURCHILL

ICECREAM

N
H
ℬ

A Royal Court Programme / Text published by

NICK HERN BOOKS

riginal
sion of Walker Books
£11 5HJ

Icecream copyright © 1989 by Caryl Churchill

Extract from *Brigadoon* by Lerner & Lowe:
© 1948, United Artists Music Corp, USA
Reproduced by permission of Sam Fox Pub Co (London)
Ltd, London WC2H 0EA

Set in Baskerville
by Book Ens, Saffron Walden, Essex
Printed by Expression Printers Limited,
London N7 9DP

British Library Cataloguing in Publication Data

Churchill, Caryl
  Icecream
  I. Title
  822'914

ISBN 1 85459 016 2

Caution
All rights whatsoever in this play are strictly reserved.
Requests to reproduce the text in whole or in part should
be addressed to the publisher. Application for performance
in any medium or for translation into any language should
be made to Margaret Ramsay Limited, 14a Goodwin's
Court, St Martin's Lane, London WC2N 4LL. No
performances may be given unless a licence has been
obtained prior to rehearsals.

The Royal Court Theatre
presents
ICECREAM
BY CARYL CHURCHILL

LANCE	husband	Philip Jackson
	and	
VERA	wife	Carole Hayman
PHIL	brother	David Thewlis
	and	
JAQ	sister	Saskia Reeves

Man in Devon, Shrink, Fellow Guest, Hitcher, Professor .... Allan Corduner

Waitress, Drunk Woman, Hitcher's Mother, South American Woman Passenger ..... Gillian Hanna

There will be no interval

Directed by	Max Stafford-Clark
Designed by	Peter Hartwell
Costumes designed by	Jennifer Cook
Lighting by	Christopher Toulmin
Sound by	Bryan Bowen
Voice Coach	Sally Grace
Assistant Directors	Melanie Kenyon
	Tamsin Oglesby
Costume Supervisor	Cathie Skilbeck
Stage Manager	Fleur Howard
Deputy Stage Manager	Fiona Bardsley
Assistant Stage Manager	Gary Crant
Student Assistant Stage Manager	Susan Chory

Wardrobe care by PERSIL and BIO-TEX. Adhesive by COPYDEX and EVODE LTD. Ioniser for the lighting control room by THE LONDON IONISER CENTRE (836 0211). Cordless drill by MAKITA ELECTRIC (UK) LTD. Watches by THE TIMEX CORPORATION. Batteries by EVER READY. Refrigerators by ELECTROLUX and PHILLIPS MAJOR APPLIANCES LTD. Microwaves by TOSHIBA UK LTD. Kettles for rehearsals by MORPHY RICHARDS. Video for casting purposes by HITACHI. Cold bottled beers at the bar supplied by YOUNG & CO. BREWERY, WANDSWORTH. Coffee machines by CONA.

FINANCIALLY ASSISTED BY THE
ROYAL BOROUGH OF
KENSINGTON AND CHELSEA

BIOGRAPHIES

CARYL CHURCHILL — At the Royal Court : *Owners* (1972), *Objections to Sex and Violence* (1975), *Light Shining in Buckinghamshire* (Joint Stock 1976), *Traps* (1977), *Cloud Nine* (Joint Stock 1979 and 1981), *Three More Sleepless Nights* (Soho Poly 1981), *Top Girls* (1982), *Fen* (Joint Stock 1983), *A Mouthful of Birds* (with DAVID LAN, Joint Stock 1986), *Serious Money* (1987).

JENNIFER COOK — Resident Wardrobe Supervisor at the Royal Court for the last 5 years. For the Royal Court: The Edward Bond Season, *Aunt Dan and Lemon* (and Public Theater, New York). Other theatre credits include: Resident designer at RADA; five years at Footsbarn Theatre, Cornwall; several Off-Broadway shows; *A Lovely Sunday for Creve Coeur* (Old Red Lion). Costume work includes: Kenyon Festival Ohio; Julliard School; New York Shakespeare Festival.

ALLAN CORDUNER — For the Royal Court : *No End of Blame*, *Serious Money* (Wyndhams, Public, and Royale Theater, New York). Other theatre credits include: *Measure for Measure* (Birmingham, National Theatre), *The Amazons and the Entertainer* (The Actor's Company), *The Police* (Roundhouse), *Once a Catholic* (Wyndhams), *Traitors* (Drill Hall), *Milkwood Blues* (Lyric, Hammersmith). Television credits include: *Diamonds, Roots, Freud, Cold Warrior, Girls on Top, Mandela*. Films include: *Bad Medicine, Yentl, Hearts of Fire, Talk Radio, Fat Man and Little Boy* (to be released).

PETER HARTWELL — For the Royal Court: *The Glad Hand, Wheelchair Willie, Not Quite Jerusalem, The Genius, A Colder Climate, The Arbor*, The Edward Bond Season, *Operation Bad Apple, The Grass Widow, The Recruiting Officer, Our Country's Good*. At the Royal Court and Public Theater New York: *Rat in the Skull, Top Girls, Aunt Dan and Lemon, Serious Money* (also on Broadway). At the Theatre Upstairs: *An Empty Desk, Marie and Bruce, Seduced*. For Joint Stock: *Epsom Downs, Cloud Nine, The Ragged Trousered Philanthropists, Borderline, Crimes of Vautrin*. Other theatre includes: *She Stoops to Conquer, The Beaux' Stratagem* (Lyric, Hammersmith); *Serjeant Musgrave's Dance* (National); *Delicatessen* (Half Moon Theatre). Also work for Hampstead Theatre Club, Foco Novo, Newcastle and Liverpool Playhouses and the Canadian Stage Company Toronto.

GILLIAN HANNA — Theatre includes: *A Common Woman, Elizabeth: Almost by Chance, Sweeney Todd*, (All for the Half Moon); *Duet for One, Wuthering Heights, Who's Afraid of Virginia Woolf?* (all for the Crucible, Sheffield); *Curtains* (Hampstead), *The House of Bernarda Alba* (Lyric, Hammersmith and Globe), *Scum, Vinegar Tom, Origin of the Species* (Monstrous Regiment). Television includes: *All Creatures Great and Small* (Horizon docudrama). Films include: *Wolves of Willoughby Chase*.Translations include: *Elizabeth: Almost by Chance a Woman, One Woman Plays*, original translation of *Accidental Death of an Anarchist, Dialogue Between a Prostitute and One of Her Clients* (all from Italian); *Shakespeare's Sister* (from French).

CAROLE HAYMAN — At the Royal Court: *As Time Goes By*, *Wheelchair Willie*, *Cloud Nine* (Joint Stock), *Top Girls*, *Sugar and Spice*, *Magnificence*, *Light Shining in Buckinghamshire* (Joint Stock). Directed at the Royal Court: *Ripen Our Darkness*, *Bazaar and Rummage*, *The Great Celestial Cow* (Joint Stock), *Shirley*, *Byrthrite*. Other theatre includes: *Hitler Dances*, *Amalfi* (Traverse Theatre); *Fanshen*, *Speakers* (Joint Stock). Television includes: *Upline*, *Howard's Way*, *Dancers*, *Lytton's Diary*, *Roger Doesn't Live Here Anymore*, *Widows*, *Omnibus* (on Caryl Churchill). Films include: *Lady Jane*. Writing credits include work on television and radio and a novel, *All the Best, Kim* which was serialised on Radio 4.

PHILIP JACKSON — For the Royal Court: *Dick Whittington*, *Live Like Pigs*, *Rat in the Skull* (also Public Theater, New York). Other theatre includes: *The Oven Glove Murders*, *The Fosdyke Saga*, (Bush); *A Midsummer Night's Dream* (RSC), *Serjeant Musgrave's Dance*, *The Passion* (National); *Comedians* (Nottingham Playhouse), *Rooted* (Hampstead), *Into Europe* (Lyric, Hammersmith). Television includes: *The Storyteller*, *The Dark Room*, *Our Geoff*, *Lizzie's Pictures*, *On the Palm*, *Farmer's Arms*, *Pasmore*, *Games Without Frontiers*, *Blooming Youth*, *Glamour Night*, *Pennies from Heaven*, *Robin of Sherwood*, *Poirot*. Films include: *The Fourth Protocol*, *Give My Regards to Broad Street*, *Scum*, *High Hopes*.

SASKIA REEVES — Theatre includes: *The Attractions* (Soho Poly), *Measure for Measure*, *Who's Afraid of Virginia Woolf?*, (Young Vic); *The Man of Mode*, *A Midsummer Night's Dream* (Cheek by Jowl); *Infidelities* (Lyric, Hammersmith); *Separation*, *Smelling a Rat* (Hampstead); *Twelfth Night* (Royal Exchange, Manchester). Television includes: *Metamorphosis*, *A Woman of Substance*, *Lytton's Diary*, *Last Day of Summer*.

DAVID THEWLIS — Theatre includes: *The Ruffian on the Stair*, *The Wooley* (Redgrave, Farnham), *Buddy Holly at the Regal* (New Vic). Television includes: *Picture Friend*, *Only Fools and Horses*, *Radio Pictures*, *Up the Elephant and Round the Castle*, *The Bill*, *Valentine Park*, *The Singing Detective*, *Road*, *A Bit of a Do*. Films include: *Little Dorritt*, *Short and Curlies*, *Vroom*, *Deep Red Instant Love*, *Resurrected*.

CHRISTOPHER TOULMIN — Resident Lighting Designer at the Royal Court for 7 years. For the Royal Court: *Falkland Sound*, *Aunt Dan and Lemon*, *The Grace of Mary Traverse*, *Ourselves Alone*, *Road*, *A Lie of the Mind*, *The Recruiting Officer*. Other theatre includes: *The Seagull* (Sherman, Cardiff), *Gaudete* (Almeida), *Cosi Fan Tutte* (Scottish Opera), *Mary Stuart* (Greenwich), *School for Scandal* (Bristol Old Vic), *Ghost Sonata* (Opera Factory), *Roots*, *The Father*, *Bed* (National Theatre); *Making History* (Field Day, National Theatre), several productions at Liverpool Playhouse.

NICHOLAS WRIGHT ON THE OPENING OF THE THEATRE UPSTAIRS

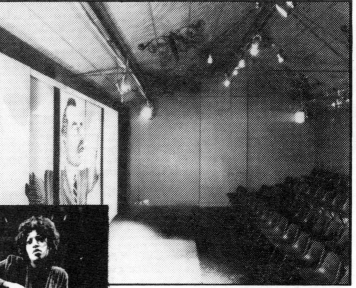

1969   Set for THE ENOCH SHOW.

1970   AC/DC by Heathcote Williams.
Victor Henry, Sheila Scott-Wilkinson.

1971   CAPTAIN JACK'S REVENGE
by Michael Smith.
Michael Pennington.

It started as a rehearsal room. There's a photograph of Bernard Shaw during rehearsals there of *Androcles and the Lion*. It's an early 'photo-opportunity' with the famous author waving a sword in the air, supposedly showing the actors how to do it.

During the George Devine years it was run by Clement Freud as a nightclub. It was a typical dive of the period, complete with upperclass drunks and a pocket-handkerchief-sized dance-floor — the kind of place you see, usually called 'The Green Cockatoo', in old Edgar Wallace movies.

Under Bill Gaskill it continued as a club under the Court's own management, an enterprise which ended in a mysterious fire. It was around this time that the room began to turn, gradually and by phases, into a theatre.

The first performances were free and semi-private. There was neither stage, set nor lighting and nobody got paid. Helen Montagu, who was the Court's General Manager, would tell directors "Your budget's nothing". "When you say 'nothing' — " one of them mildly asked, "how small exactly is it? Five pounds?" "It's nothing! *Nothing!*" she replied, shrieking with laughter.

From those days I remember a very early Mike Leigh play, invisible behind a sea of craning necks; Jack Shepherd and Deborah Norton in a Sam Shepard one-acter; Bill Bryden, Barry Hanson and Gaskill himself all wearing Jill Bennett masks.

It was the late 1960's and the spirit which had already transformed painting and popular music was beginning to change the theatre. The idea of turning what we still called "the club" into an experimental theatre was very much a part of this. It grew out of conversations mainly between Gaskill and Peter Gill. Peter imagined a studio space like those where New York artists showed their work-in-progress. Bill, more pragmatic, wanted full productions, normal deadlines, first-nights, reviews and runs — and this is what happened.

In a way the Theatre Upstairs replaced the by now very expensive 'New Play Seasons' Bill had staged downstairs in the main theatre. The Court used to present classic plays as a matter of course, so putting on three or four new plays in a row was regarded as pretty exceptional — the posters advertised the plays as "New!!" complete with exclamation marks.

The second and last of these seasons had featured a play — a light and fantastical comedy by David Cregan called *The Houses by the Green* — for which I, as assistant director, had compiled a programme so wildly inappropriate (full of facts and figures about bad housing) that the critics reviewed it more fully than the play. I stayed at home expecting to get the sack. When Bill rang me up I was not surprised. When he said he'd raised the money to turn the club into a studio theatre and that he wanted me to run it I was stunned.

The plan was that the Theatre Upstairs (the name had been suggested by Dick Linklater of the Arts Council) would open with a season of four plays and that more would follow if these were successful. They were not — and the fourth, an early stab at political revue entitled *The Enoch Show* managed without ever actually opening to accrue a legendary reputation for awfulness. "It's so bad it's actually rather sweet", David Hare said. But once started there was no going back. Bill's criticism in private was savage but he swung the money once again and the work continued.

Peter Gill had just finished a short play called *Over Gardens Out*. I thought it was marvellous. I also knew that Peter understood this new theatre we'd created, the physical space of it. He and I had shared an extraordinary moment a few months earlier, before the builders had begun to convert it. Noticing that the walls and roof seemed not to add up, we'd climbed out of a window and up several roofs to find ourselves peering through a small semi-circular window into an attic space at the top of the Theatre-Upstairs-to-be, intersected by a row of ornamental iron roof-supports. We realised that the ceiling could be removed, that there'd be space for lamps to be rigged and that the ironwork would give it all atmosphere (as it does to this day). It was at that moment that it seemed to change from being a jumped-up rehearsal space into a theatre. So in asking Peter to direct his play I was also asking him to turn the vision we'd shared into something real: a production.

What he did was simple but in some ways very surprising. The theatre was stripped almost bare: it looked light and airy. There was a huge acting-area which somehow seemed to envelop the whole room. There was no wing-space or masking, no sense of actors waiting offstage to enter. In fact there was no offstage at all. Two television sets emitted whatever programmes happened to be on — a random element. Most striking, the windows were opened, so that the audience found itself looking over the rooftops of Belgravia. It was summer,and when James Hazeldine and Don Hawkins as the two adolescent boys of Peter's story perched on a window sill and chatted a real sun used to set directly behind them — a breathtaking image of youth and evanescence.

Later productions Upstairs were to be scenically very elaborate, even spectacular — but in my own mind at least they evolved from this stripped-down vision of a room in which the space was unashamedly shared between the audience and actors and where all the elements were real.

Bill defined the ideal relationship between the main theatre and the Theatre Upstairs as "paternal", so Oedipal tensions were inevitable. Another early production, Howard Brenton's first full-length play *Revenge*, revealed the width of the crevasse. One director collared me on the stairs, his nose wrinkled in incredulity. "You don't *really* think that play's any good, do you?" I said that I did, that I thought it was excellent. He walked away shaking his head in pity; clearly I'd fallen prey to some baleful influence.

Caryl Churchill's play *Owners* came fifty or so productions later. Every play had produced a crisis of some kind: with *Owners* it came when Jill Bennett, who was appearing in person this time, broke her ankle in a minor car accident the day before the dress-rehearsal. ("Is there anything I can do?" asked her then husband, who had been driving. "I think you've done quite enough for one day," she replied politely.)

By this time the Theatre Upstairs had been going for nearly four years; for a year of this time it had been run by Roger Croucher, for the rest of this time it had been run by me. It was a difficult theatre to run only in the sense that there was never enough money, that everything was done on the cheap and that people who worked there were uniformly exploited. But I never had the slightest doubt that artistically this was the most exciting and important theatre in London, that I'd been blessed by fortune. I was not of course objective — but I think anyone looking at the list of plays which were produced there would agree that something very extraordinary had happened.

1972 OWNERS by Caryl Churchill.
(Her first play at the Royal Court)
David Swift, Jill Bennett.

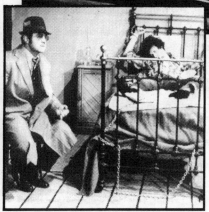

1973 ROCKY HORROR SHOW by Richard O'Brien.
Tim Curry.

1974 GEOGRAPHY OF A HORSE DREAMER
by Sam Shepard.
Bob Hoskins, Stephen Rea.

One reason, I now believe, was not that the playwrights were any better or more numerous than they are now, but that the theatre was better subsidised. It was a time of "slots to fill" — which play should it be, what the hell can we put on next? Plays got produced which were by no means everybody's favourite, and often these odd, intuitive risks worked better — were newer and more striking — than the first choices.

True, there were other factors. We were the Royal Court, we were there, we attracted the best, or most of it. The spirit of the times was confident. Money went further. An openhanded and credulous DHSS subsidised many fine first plays. There were no 'workshops' or 'rehearsed readings' of the kind which now so plague and discourage young writers.

But mainly there was — Upstairs and in other theatres too — a genuine demand for new work. And this demand created opportunity. Playwrights were encouraged and heartened and the result was a golden age.

NICHOLAS WRIGHT

Nicholas Wright joined the English Stage Company in 1967 as casting director; in the following year he directed a Sunday night production of his own play *Changing Lines*. He was joint artistic director at the Royal Court (with Robert Kidd) from 1975-77. Currently Literary Manager of the National Theatre, his play *Mrs Klein* is running at the Apollo Theatre in West End.

MAX STAFFORD-CLARK ON THE CLOSING OF THE THEATRE UPSTAIRS

The Royal Court seems to have been chronically underfunded for so long that, if music-hall were still around, we would be a music-hall joke; The Fulham FC of the theatrical world. Even our supporters are entitled to ask if the situation is really so serious. After all, we've survived so far. Sure, we produce half the work we did 15 years ago, but we've survived. Is it really necessary to close the Theatre Upstairs, or is it simply a dramatic gesture designed to enlist support?

1986

ROAD by Jim Cartwright.
Susan Brown.
Jim Cartwright's first play started at the Theatre Upstairs, transferred to the Main House, and then to New York. It was also filmed for television. His second play, BED, is now running at the National Theatre

The truth is that 3 years ago we were already approaching the point where it would be hard to present a full year's work of 4 plays on the Main Stage and four plays in the Theatre Upstairs. On this occasion, Joseph Papp responded to our plight with a $50,000 Challenge Fund: a dollar for every pound we raised. That year (1985/6), with his contribution, we raised £113,000 towards our annual revenue. In the two years since then, THE NORMAL HEART and SERIOUS MONEY both played to capacity business and both transferred to the West End. The Royal Court made £75,000 from the ten month run of SERIOUS MONEY in 1987/8. This year, there has been no comparable box-office hit and the vulnerable nature of the Royal Court's position stands revealed. The 1½% increase in Arts Council funding we have been told to expect, means a further cut of £30,000 in real terms and, once again, the moment has arisen where I am unable to present a full year's work in both theatres.

As I write, we have taken the decision to close the Theatre Upstairs for up to six months, while we discuss our situation with the Arts Council and explore possible alternatives. To close the Theatre Upstairs permanently would be a disaster for the Royal Court and bad for English theatre as a whole: Timberlake Wertenbaker, Jim Cartwright, Sarah Daniels and Caryl Churchill are a few of its recent graduates. The Theatre Upstairs enables us to sustain writers through their apprenticeship. Any theatre in the country would be glad to present the next play by Caryl Churchill or Timberlake Wertenbaker. Their work is sought after by film and television companies: it is our ability to place writers in this position in the first place that is under threat. Closing the Theatre Upstairs should only be seen as an immediate short-term solution; it is such an essential part of our work that, in the future, I would rather close altogether than encourage anyone to think that it can be an expendable component of the Royal Court's operation.

For the last 5 years, we have been caught in an argument between the Arts Council, who seek plural funding for their clients, and the Royal Borough of Kensington and Chelsea, who see the Royal Court as a

1987
SERIOUS MONEY
by Caryl Churchill.
Gary Oldman,
Linda Bassett,
Alfred Molina.

PHOTO: JOHN HAYNES

1987
THE EMPEROR by Ryszard Kapuscinski,
adapted by Michael Hastings and Jonathan Miller.
(Transferred from Upstairs to the Main House)
Stefan Kalipha, Hepburn Graham,
Okon Jones, Ben Onwukwe.

national resource, which should be funded nationally. Both sides have a
point. The Royal Court clearly does have a national role, but then so do
the English National Opera or the London Festival Ballet; both of them
are funded to the tune of over £1 million annually by the City of
Westminster, hardly a council of radical communards. Meanwhile, the
Royal Borough of Kensington and Chelsea have consistently refused the
level of support which might be appropriate if we were no more than a
local asset. The victims of this argument are the Royal Court and the
writing community we seek to serve. At the same time, our funding
position relative to other theatres has declined. In 1983/4, the Royal
Court received the third highest subsidy in the country from the Arts
Council of Great Britain, behind only the National and the RSC. In the
current year, we are seventh; while in an overall table of public funding
from all sources — ACGB, regional and local — we have dropped from
7th to 16th. We now receive total public funding on a level with Derby
Playhouse and the York Theatre Royal; less than Greenwich, less than
Coventry and less than the Lyric, Hammersmith. Not that our sister
theatres don't merit this level of funding, my point is that this is what
it costs to run a major theatre. As public subsidy has dropped we have
become increasingly dependent on raising money. Over the last five
years, we've raised a higher proportion of our turnover than any other
theatre in the country, except the National Theatre. The Olivier Appeal
has so far raised nearly £190,000 for capital redevelopment. None of this
however diminishes the risky nature of new work and the volatile
behaviour of our box-office despite record-breaking years in 1986 and
1987. In fact, there's a danger that we've become so committed to
incentive-funding, marketing and fund-raising that it's become heretical
to state what is obvious commonsense — that without an equal
commitment from the public sector, the Royal Court cannot continue as
a major national resource for new writing.

It's ironic that this is happening at a time when the Royal Court's reputation at home and international standing abroad is so high. Our association with Joseph Papp has led to the presentation of five plays in seven years in New York, and we are about to undertake a tour to Sydney and Toronto of OUR COUNTRY'S GOOD and THE RECRUITING OFFICER. The newly affluent British Council have a fresh enthusiasm about taking new work abroad. I hope we will have it to give to them. At home, we usually do pretty well in the Awards Season. We have won the Olivier Award for Best Play two years running, with work that has been generated from workshops within the Royal Court: SERIOUS MONEY by Caryl Churchill in 1987 and OUR COUNTRY'S GOOD by Timberlake Wertenbaker in 1988. Closure of the Theatre Upstairs will also come at a time when we have a particularly lively repertoire of work by promising writers in hand. Clare McIntyre, Harwant Bains, Victoria Hardie and Fred D'Aguiar are hardly known at the moment. They are likely to remain unknown and unperformed if the closure of the Theatre Upstairs continues on a permanent basis. "Is The Credit of Our Age nothing? Must our present times pass away unnoticed by posterity?" wrote a desperate young playwright. This cry of agony came from Oliver Goldsmith writing in 1773 when market forces swelled Drury Lane's capacity to the extent that new writing had become too risky to contemplate.

As Mr Palumbo prepares to take up the helm in April, he exchanges the choppy waters of architectural controversy for the full force gale of a life in the Arts. He has a difficult job. I recall him saying that excellence would be rewarded and centres of excellence would not be allowed to decline. I understand the enormous pressure on the Arts Council but, despite the acknowledgement in both The Glory of the Garden and The Cork Report of the vital developmental role played by theatres who specialise in new writing, we have fallen way behind. One only has to look back five years to see a far more vigorous and confident contribution from the new writing theatres. Five years from now the spectre is chilling; the National Theatre will become outstanding as the rest of us struggle to produce half our current output. It will become a lone bastion of culture in its riverbank fortress, guarded by prestige from attrition. A modest and tamed RSC will just about be keeping its head above water, while the rest of us will have become well-nigh invisible: no longer able to produce work that would justify our existence. Meanwhile, in the upper rooms of pubs, unpaid actors will appear in yet more productions of Shakespeare, in a desperate effort to display their talents. I've seen this future for theatre. It's called New York. It doesn't work.

I believe that now is the moment for the Arts Council of Great Britain to respond and fund the Royal Court properly, as a national resource. After all, our theatre will be known to posterity by the plays we have created, everything else dies with us. On these grounds the Royal Court is arguably the *most* important theatre in the country: certainly not the sixteenth.

Max Stafford-Clark
ARTISTIC DIRECTOR OF THE ROYAL COURT THEATRE
7 March 1989

SUPPORTERS OF THE ROYAL COURT
JOIN US !

For many years now Members of the Royal Court Theatre Society have received special notice of new productions, but why not become a **Friend, Associate** or a **Patron of the Royal Court**, thereby involving yourself directly in maintaining the high standard and unique quality of Royal Court productions — while enjoying complimentary tickets to the shows themselves?

1 MEMBERSHIP SCHEME

For £10 you will receive details of all forthcoming events via the Royal Court *Member's Letter*, and be entitled to purchase any available seat for £3 during previews and other selected performances (maximum of two per Member).

2 FRIENDS OF THE ROYAL COURT

For £35 (or £50 joint membership) you will be entitled to one (or two) complimentary ticket(s) for performances on the Main Stage and one (or two) tickets for productions in the Theatre Upstairs. You will automatically be on our mailing list and be invited to all productions lectures and special events, via the friend's letter.

3 ASSOCIATES OF THE ROYAL COURT

For £350 you will be entitled to four top price tickets to all Main House productions and four tickets to all plays in the Theatre Upstairs.

4 PATRONS OF THE ROYAL COURT

For £1,000 you can make a 'personal appearance' on a plaque in the Royal Court lobby, and appear in our programme. In addition, you will be entitled to six free tickets for shows in the Main House or the Theatre Upstairs.

When you have chosen from the four categories, please make your cheque/ P.O. payable to the *Royal Court Theatre Society* and send to: *Max Stafford-Clark, Artistic Director, Royal Court Theatre, Sloane Square, London SW1*. Alternatively, if you wish to covenant for four years or more we — as a registered charity — can claim back the tax you have already paid, thereby increasing the value of your donation; forms are available from the above address.

PHOTO: SNOWDON

Laurence Olivier as Archie Rice
in John Osborne's THE ENTERTAINER

THE OLIVIER APPEAL
Patron: Lord Olivier

The Appeal was launched in June 1988 — The Royal Court's 100th anniversary year. The target is £800,000 to repair and refurbish the theatre and to enable the English Stage Company to maintain and continue its worldwide reputation as Britain's 'National Theatre of new writing'.

The Royal Court would like to thank the following for their generous contributions to the Appeal:

Andrew Bainbridge
Associated British Foods
The Clifford Barclay Trust
Peter Carter
Graham Cowley
David Crosner
The Douglas Heath Eves Trust
Douglas Fairbanks
The Economist
The Esmee Fairbairn Trust
Evans and Reiss
Robert Fleming Bank
D J Freeman & Company
Brian Friel
Gala (100th Anniversary)
The Godinton Trust
Caroline Goodall
Lord Goodman
Christopher Hampton

Hatter (IMO) Foundation
The Hedley Trust
The John Lewis Partnership
The Kobler Trust
The London and Edinburgh Trust
The Mercers
National Westminster Bank
Anna Louise Neuberg Trust
Olivier Banquet
Pirelli Ltd.
A.J.R. Purssell
St. Quentin Ltd.
The Rayne Foundation
The Lord Sainsbury Trust
D. R. Slack
W.H. Smith & Son
Max Stafford-Clark
'Stormy Monday' Charity Premiere
Andrew Wadsworth
Womens Playhouse Trust

FOR THE ROYAL COURT

DIRECTION
Artistic Director.. MAX STAFFORD-CLARK
Deputy Director.. SIMON CURTIS
Casting Director..LISA MAKIN
Literary Manager ....KATE HARWOOD
Assistant Director..PHILIP HOWARD
Artistic Assistant .... MELANIE KENYON

PRODUCTION
Production Manager ....BO BARTON
Chief Electrician ....COLIN ROXBOROUGH
Electrician.. DENIS O'HARE*
Sound Designer...BRYAN BOWEN
Board Operators.. BENI TURKSON*, STEVE HEPWORTH*
Master Carpenter .... CHRIS BAGUST
Deputy Master Carpenter...ALAN JOYCE
Wardrobe Supervisor ....JENNIFER COOK
Deputy Wardrobe Supervisor...CATHIE SKILBECK

ADMINISTRATION
General Manager..GRAHAM COWLEY
Assistant to General Manager.. LUCY WOOLLATT
Finance Administrator..STEPHEN MORRIS
Press (730 2652)... SALLY LYCETT
Finance Assistant .... RACHEL HARRISON
Marketing & Publicity Manager .... GUY CHAPMAN
Development Director...TOM PETZAL
Development Assistant .... JACQUELINE VIEIRA
House Manager ....WILLIAM DAY
Deputy House Manager ....ALISON SMITH
Box Office Manager...GILL RUSSELL
Box Office Assistants... GERALD BROOKING, RITA SHARMA
Stage Door/Telephonists .... ANGELA TOULMIN, JAN NOYCE*
Evening Stage Door ....TYRONE LUCAS*
Maintenance..JOHN LORRIGIO*
Cleaners...EILEEN CHAPMAN*, IVY JONES*
Firemen ....PAUL KLEINMANN*, DAVID WYATT*

YOUNG PEOPLE'S THEATRE
Director .... ELYSE DODGSON
Administrator ....DOMINIC TICKELL
Youth and Community Worker .... EUTON DALY

*Part-time staff

COUNCIL: Chairman: MATTHEW EVANS, CHRIS BAGUST, BO BARTON, STUART BURGE, ANTHONY C. BURTON, CARYL CHURCHILL, BRIAN COX, HARRIET CRUICKSHANK, SIMON CURTIS, ALLAN DAVIS, DAVID LLOYD DAVIS, ROBERT FOX, MRS. HENNY GESTETNER OBE, DEREK GRANGER, DAVID HARE, JOCELYN HERBERT, DAVID KLEEMAN, HANIF KUREISHI, SONIA MELCHETT, JAMES MIDGLEY, JOAN PLOWRIGHT CBE, GREVILLE POKE, RICHARD PULFORD, JANE RAYNE, JIM TANNER, SIR HUGH WILLATT.

This Theatre is associated with the Regional Theatre Young Directors Scheme.

COMING NEXT

IN THE MAIN HOUSE   730 1745

From 1st June

The Royal Court Theatre
in association with Mayfest presents

AMERICAN BAGPIPES by Iain Heggie

Directed by Lindsay Posner. Designed by Julian McGowan.

AMERICAN BAGPIPES, a hilarious farce dealing with the reunion of a Scottish family, portrays family life at its sharpest and funniest. Winner of the 1988 John Whiting Award, AMERICAN BAGPIPES will be seen as part of Mayfest before its London premiere at the Royal Court.

"a powerful, quirky, funny and virtually Euripdean domestic comedy that surprises as much as it delights". Financial Times.

From 5th July

JGN Productions and the LIFT Festival
in association with the Royal Court Theatre
present the Abbey Theatre production of

A WHISTLE IN THE DARK by Tom Murphy

Directed by Garry Hynes. Designed by Brien Vahey.

A WHISTLE IN THE DARK traces the struggle of an Irish immigrant family at war with themselves and the English culture in which they now live. Tom Murphy's reputation stands high in Ireland, although his work is rarely seen in London.Garry Hynes' production of his CONVERSATIONS ON A HOMECOMING played to critical accolades at the Donmar Warehouse in 1987.

"Directed with quiet relentless intensity by Garry Hynes... frightening power" The Observer

From 3rd August

The Royal Court Theatre and Diana Bliss present

The triumphant return of

THE RECRUITING OFFICER by George Farquhar
AND
OUR COUNTRY'S GOOD by Timberlake Wertenbaker

Based on Thomas Keneally's novel 'The Playmaker.

IN REPERTOIRE

Directed by Max Stafford-Clark. Designed by Peter Hartwell.

Farquhar's classic comedy THE RECRUITING OFFICER plays in repertoire with OUR COUNTRY'S GOOD by Timberlake Wertenbaker. OUR COUNTRY'S GOOD won the BBC Award for the West End Play of the Year — Laurence Olivier Awards 1988, and the 1988 Evening Standard Drama Award for 'The Most Promising Playwright'.

"A moving experience... coupling this lovely workwith Farquhar's THE RECRUITING OFFICER was a brilliant concept by Max Stafford-Clark". The Standard.

ICECREAM

First preview: 6 April 1989
Press night: 11 April 1989

Characters

LANCE ⎫
VERA ⎬ husband and wife, American, around 40

PHIL ⎫
JAQ ⎬ brother and sister, English, twenties

MAN IN DEVON
SHRINK
COLLEAGUE
FELLOW GUEST
DRUNK WOMAN
HITCHER
HITCHER'S MOTHER
PROFESSOR
SOUTH AMERICAN WOMAN PASSENGER

The first ten scenes are set in the UK during a
summer in the late eighties, the second ten in the US
the following year.

Notes on layout

A speech usually follows the one immediately before it
BUT:

1) When one character starts speaking before the other
    has finished, the point of interruption is marked/

e.g.

LANCE.	Are you not in touch / with a great many relatives?
VERA.	Or maybe just plain cousins because what's Lance's is mine, I mean third, third cousins.

2) A character sometimes continues speaking right
    through another's speech:

e.g.

LANCE.	You can't help loving England. The green fields. The accents. The pubs. / I mean people
VERA.	Pubs are so great.
LANCE.	are violent and stupid, that's all. It's just life.

3) Sometimes a speech follows on from a speech earlier
    than the one immediately before it, and continuity is
    marked*

e.g.

VERA.	In what / condition*
LANCE.	Don't discuss it. We are not giving you any money.
JAQ.	*Give me a thousand dollars and I'll have it serviced.

where LANCE's 'Don't discuss it' is cued by VERA's
'In what' and JAQ's 'Give me a thousand' is cued by
VERA's 'condition'.

4) Double columns are used to indicate two sequences
    which run independently.

e.g.

LANCE.	Last summer.	PHIL.	He was a very evil man. I don't like evil.

I   UK

1. Road to the Isles

LANCE *and* VERA *in car. They are singing.*

LANCE   The far coo-oolins are putting love on me
& VERA.   As step I with my something to the road
           The dadeda dedadeda dedadeda away
           As step I with the sunlight for my load.
           And by something and by something and by
                                     something I will go
           And never something dadedadeda
           And something and dedadeda and something
                                              in my step
           And I'll never something something of the
                                                  isles.

           They laugh.

LANCE.   Speed bonny boat
           Like a bird on the wing
           Over the sea to Skye

VERA.   You're really flat.

           He stops.

VERA.   Sorry.

LANCE.   No, you're right.

VERA.   Oh come on.

           Pause.
           She sings.

           Why don't we go walking together
           Out beyond the valley of trees

Out where there's a hillside of heather
Curtseying gently in the breeze.
That's what I'd like to do
See the heather but with you.

It's a pity no one remembered her though.

LANCE.   My great grandmother was a very obscure woman.

VERA.   Drowning yourself in a well isn't obscure.

LANCE.   They were probably all at it.

Pause.

LANCE.   What was that from?

VERA.   Brigadoon.

LANCE.   You've got such a great memory.

2.   Castle

LANCE *is turning round looking up at ceiling.* VERA *has a guide book.*

LANCE.   What have we got that's old?

VERA.   Sofa. Freezer.

LANCE.   Nothing old. Just plenty worn out. No history.

VERA.   It's twelfth century up the end and thirteenth on top.

LANCE.   Eight hundred years. Whahey!

VERA.   I've been touching the walls to try and believe it.

LANCE.   We think the nineteenth century is history. We had wilderness and aboriginal people. For the British the nineteenth century is just now, they hardly notice it's gone. For them history is this castle. Aboriginal is before 1066. No, even

that's history, they had Alfred and the cakes.
Aboriginal is Stonehenge.

Pause. VERA *licks her fingers.*

VERA.   We do too have history.

LANCE.   Indians have their oral traditions. We can't
          claim a share in that.

VERA.   Everyone has ancestors.

LANCE.   Yes indeed and this is where they came from.
          So to that extent this is our history.

VERA.   Your history.

LANCE.   If it's mine it's yours. Like a joint bank
          account. They would all be our children's
          ancestors.

VERA.   My history's in Russia and Germany and god
          knows where.

LANCE.   Not in America anyhow because America's too
          damn recent.

          Pause.

          Do you want an icecream? Do you want an ice
          CREAM?

          Pause.

          What nobody knows isn't history.

VERA.   Just because someone doesn't know who their
          grandparents are doesn't make them not exist.
          Everyone comes from something.

LANCE.   That's evolution. I'm talking about history.

3.   Cottage

LANCE *and* VERA *outside a cottage in Devon.*
MAN *carrying chest of drawers.*

VERA.   If only we'd come to Devon first.

LANCE.   Do you know who's inherited the cottage?

MAN.   It were rented. They were waiting for her to die.

LANCE.   So what happens to it now?

MAN.   Holidays.

LANCE.   You don't know if there were any relatives mentioned in the will?

VERA.   We're not after her money. We're researching my husband's family tree.

LANCE.   Miss Glade was a cousin on his mother's side of my maternal grandfather. But I liked to think of her as Greataunt Dora.

MAN.   She didn't have any money to be after.

VERA.   Did you know her well?

MAN.   I used to do her garden when I was a boy. She had a sharp tongue but she'd give me a biscuit.

LANCE.   That's wonderful.

VERA.   Rose Cottage, Lance.

LANCE.   Maybe we could buy the chest of drawers.

4.   Flat

LANCE *and* VERA *with* PHIL *in his flat in east London.*

LANCE.   So great aunt Dora was my great /

PHIL.   was your greatgrandfather's –

LANCE.   grandmother's brother's daughter – mother's, great / grandmother's –

PHIL.   – mother's, right,

LANCE: she was my greatgrand*mother's* brother's daughter and your greatgrand / *father's*

PHIL.   father's

LANCE.   brother's daughter.

PHIL.   So they were both / the brothers, the brother and *sister* of –

LANCE.   So looking at it another way they were the brother and sister of Dora's father, who was Albert. So there's / Henry, Albert and

PHIL.   Albert, Henry . . .

LANCE.   Mavis, / a sister and two brothers, the

PHIL.   Mavis, that's good.

LANCE.   children of William and Jane who was born, *William* was born in eighteen ten, we're going back one hundred and eighty years, and he was a shoemaker in York and Dora's / grandfather.

PHIL.   That's my great . . .

LANCE.   Your great *great* grandfather, because your greatgrandfather was Henry, who had five children / one of whom –

PHIL.   And who went to America?

LANCE.   Wait, let me, / one of those five children was

VERA.   Lance's grandfather.

LANCE.   your grandmother – yes my grandfather, that's
          Thomas, who was the son of Mavis and Frank
          who drank himself to death, Thomas sailed
          from Bristol in nineteen oh two and settled /in
          Michigan.

PHIL.   And made his fortune.

LANCE.   No, unfortunately I would say no.

PHIL.   Are you frightened of dogs?

VERA.   No, that's fine, I, no, German shepherds, it's
          stupid, / I know he won't –

PHIL.   No, you're right to be frightened, that's what
          he's for, a deterrent, I count on it, scares the
          shit – some people just put up a sign in the
          window but I do actually have one because I
          think people find you out and then they really
          go for you.

VERA.   So is he very fierce?

PHIL.   No, you could put a baby on his plate.

VERA.   But if someone attacked you?

PHIL.   I hope so or what's the point of the food bill?

LANCE.   So your grandmother, did you say Madge?

PHIL.   I think it was Madge. Unless it was Elsie. Let's
          go for Madge.

LANCE.   So Madge and Thomas and Dora, that's
          Thomas who went to America, were all first
          cousins. And Thomas was my mother's father
          and Madge was your father's mother / so they

PHIL.   father's, yes

LANCE.   were second cousins, second cousins, yes, and
          that makes you and me one down from that is
          third cousins.

PHIL.   Is that how it works? what about removed? /
          Cousin once –

LANCE. No. that's if you take say Dora and your father, if you go another generation / up or down you get . . .

PHIL. So we're third cousins and you're (*To* VERA.) my third cousin in law. / I don't even know

VERA. I guess.

PHIL. my first cousins.

LANCE. Are you not in touch / with a great many relatives?

VERA. Or maybe just plain cousins because what's Lance's is mine, I mean third, third cousins.

PHIL. Sorry, what?

VERA. Nothing, sorry.

LANCE. With other relatives, are you in touch with –?

PHIL. I have a sister. She's out.

LANCE. And your parents?

PHIL. Both alas deceased.

VERA. I'm sorry.

PHIL. No, well, a long time.

LANCE. So what about aunts and uncles?

PHIL. I had a loony uncle in Brighton but he shot himself. That was on my mother's side.

VERA. Do you not like family?

PHIL. I quite fancy Americans.

LANCE. Well I'm certainly very glad we found you. It's a great thrill for us.

Pause.

PHIL. Shall we go for a curry?

5. **Pub**

LANCE *and* VERA *drinking with* PHIL *and* JAQ.

JAQ.   Paper round, busker, Tesco, toy factory, jeans
                  shop, Woolworth, winebar, van driver,
                  pavement artist, singer with a rock group,
                  photographer's assistant, office cleaner,
                  primary school teacher, drug pusher, vet's
                  receptionist, journalist, cleaning chickens,
                  hospital orderly, gardener, carpenter, my
                  friend's dress shop, traffic warden, tourist
                  guide, hypnotherapist, motorbike messenger,
                  frozen peas, stall in the market, plumber's
                  mate, computer programmer, translator,
                  escapologist, and five secretarial.

VERA.   You make me feel so boring.

JAQ.   Whereas Phil never worked / – never had a job

PHIL.   Ah.

JAQ.   in his life, never had to get up / in the

PHIL.   I do always get up.

JAQ.   morning, never had to get up.

VERA.   I do get bored but it doesn't occur to me to
                  just – not that being a dental assistant is as
                  boring as it might sound because if you keep
                  abreast of the new technology, it's a different
                  world / almost from when I started.

PHIL.   I can't stand pain.

VERA.   You wouldn't *feel* any pain with us.

PHIL.   There's the one like a road drill and the one
                  like a jet plane and that's not two things I
                  want / in my mouth.

LANCE.   I did a great many jobs working my way
                  through college but that's some time back. I
                  worked as a lumberjack in Oregon.

PHIL.	Now Oregon –
JAQ.	The Oregon Trail.
PHIL.	The idea of Oregon, the word, just the word Oregon really thrills me. Say some more things.
LANCE.	Say –
PHIL.	Like butter pecan icecream.
VERA.	Apple pie.
PHIL.	Apple pie's not American.
VERA.	It is to us.
PHIL.	With ice cream it is.
VERA.	No with ICEcream.
LANCE.	A drug store. A soda when you're a kid / with the icecream floating.
JAQ.	Old Cadillacs. Cactus. Long straight roads.
VERA.	Yellow cabs.
PHIL.	Yellow cabs.
VERA.	Preachers on TV.
PHIL.	Preachers.
LANCE.	Hamburgers, / hotdogs.
PHIL.	Hamburgers are disgusting, we have them here thank you very much, so much American filth here, I completely loathe the United States of America.
LANCE.	I'm sorry to hear that.
PHIL.	Turn on the TV and it's American cops blowing each other through walls, this is happening all over the world. People have their own walls, they have their own policemen, they have their own guns, they have their own deaths, thank you very much. No wonder America is paranoid, you export all this filth you think someone's going to

> throw it back at you. Did you know the
> Contras think the Americans won in Vietnam
> because of Rambo?

LANCE.   I'm somewhat of a dove myself / but –

VERA.   If it's foreign policy, / if we're talking about

PHIL.   It's the essential nature of –

VERA.   the country in the world here, then
           England's / no better.

JAQ.   No one's defending England.

VERA.   The Falklands.

LANCE.   The British Empire, you can't –

PHIL.   The British and American empires.

LANCE.   There you are.

VERA.   The pot calling the kettle.

PHIL.   The slave trade. / Ireland.

VERA.   Slaves, slavery, both –

LANCE.   Ireland. Ireland.

VERA.   They are both major powers, England has
           been, America is, and it's hard, there is a
           responsibility, it's a hard position, you're up
           there to be knocked down, it's, I do feel sorry
           for the decision makers. No, they're both
           terrible countries, I guess. But America did
           stand for, at one time, when England was, it
           did stand, my people came, it must have stood
           for, a long time ago of course. No, they are
           both . . .

JAQ.   You read about Ancient Rome.

VERA.   Yes, you read where they threw the Christians
           to the lions.

JAQ.   And what will they think / when they read
           about us?

VERA.   Yes, what will they say about us?

LANCE.	But Great Britain is one thing. England is something else. And Scotland. Wales. Ireland.
JAQ.	No. Ireland is something / else again.
PHIL.	Something *else*.
LANCE.	You can't help loving England. The green fields. The accents. The pubs. / I mean people
VERA.	Pubs are so great.
LANCE.	are violent and stupid, that's all. It's just life.
JAQ.	That's shit.
VERA.	That's so negative, Lance.
LANCE.	No, it's positive. Life as in life goes on.
PHIL.	Yes, I have to admit there is still the butter pecan. Rocky road. Mocha. Blueberries and cream. Peppermint stick. / Black
VERA.	Peppermint stick yes, candy canes at Christmas on the tree, that's another . . .
PHIL.	cherry. Daiquiri. / Chocolate fudge.
LANCE.	Rum and raisin.
JAQ.	Key lime.
PHIL.	That and the movies.
	Then PHIL *notices someone in the pub.*
LANCE.	Movies, if we're talking movies – you OK?
PHIL.	Don't look now but see that man over there, /
LANCE.	Which one?
PHIL.	don't look, the ugly one, the fat –
JAQ.	Don't start / anything.
PHIL.	Start, I'm not starting, let him start, he's already / started.
LANCE.	The one in the jacket?
JAQ.	No, the shirt, the blue –

VERA.	What's he done?
PHIL.	If you want to see evil, / if you want to see
JAQ.	Phil.
PHIL.	evil that should be wiped out, just look, / just
JAQ.	Phil.
PHIL.	get him in your mind, just take care, if he's seen you with me you won't be safe / at night, just take it from me.
VERA.	Why, what?
LANCE.	What's he do, this guy?
JAQ.	Phil.
PHIL.	Don't you hate him?
JAQ.	Yes.
PHIL.	Well then.

6. Kiss

The flat.
VERA and PHIL *kiss.*

VERA.	This is a mistake.
PHIL.	OK.
VERA.	It didn't happen.
PHIL.	No problem.
VERA.	Some people do this, I don't, I never did do this, not just because of Aids, even when I was young and it was practically compulsory I was never particularly . . . it's been a relief to me that monogamy is fashionable because it was always my secret / preference.

PHIL.   Secret vice?

VERA.   No that's right, chastity, fidelity was my secret
            vice, I thought it meant I was frigid / or

PHIL.   I don't think you are.

VERA.   anyway rigid – well I'm not, but I thought I
            didn't have an appetite for life and adventure
            or I was insecure, I guess I may be insecure
            but then some of the most flamboyantly
            sexual people I've known have also been the
            most flamboyantly insecure so I don't know. I
            must be insecure right now or I wouldn't be
            talking so much.

PHIL.   It wouldn't be fair to Lance.

VERA.   It wouldn't – look I'm not even remotely
            considering. Lance adores you like I don't
            know I'd say like a son but the age difference
            is hardly, like a brother maybe, a long lost /

PHIL.   Cousin.

VERA.   brother, well yes cousin is it after all, kissing
            cousins, but Lance just is crazy about you and
            so am I which is all that was. I guess you feel
            drawn to your own flesh and blood which is
            after all why the incest taboo, you don't taboo
            things nobody wants to do, you don't taboo
            kissing the furniture. Not that the relationship
            is within the proscribed whatsits. And anyway
            you're not my flesh and blood only Lance's
            which is kind of the same thing but of course
            it's not. When I think of my European
            ancestors I see this long row of women picking
            cabbages.

PHIL.   Is that what they did?

VERA.   I've no idea, it's a cliché, I guess I think in
            clichés all the time. It's depressing but then I
            think hell, clichés are just what's true, what
            millions of people have already realised is
            true. Like proverbs are true. A stitch in time
            does in fact save nine.

PHIL.   Too many cooks do spoil the broth.

VERA.   The early bird does catch the worm.

PHIL.   Many hands do make light work. Many cooks
          do make light broth.

          They laugh.

PHIL.   Two is company and three is a crowd.

VERA.   There you are.

PHIL.   I think you're very nice.

VERA.   Good. I hope that's good?

PHIL.   It is good. I'm not at all nice. I get angry.

VERA.   You have good reason.

PHIL.   I didn't say without reason. I have bloody
          good reason, don't worry.

VERA.   That man sounds just horrible.

PHIL.   I'll probably kill him.

VERA.   Don't talk like that.

PHIL.   Don't talk, all right I won't *talk*.

VERA.   You're angry now. Don't be angry with me.

PHIL.   The trouble with relations is they're irritating.
          Nothing personal. They are irritating.

VERA.   Irritating does feel personal.

PHIL.   Not *you, Vera*, but being related.

VERA.   I kind of like it.

PHIL.   That must be nice for you.

          Pause.

VERA.   Well, there we are.

          Pause.

PHIL.   I like your ears. People will have mentioned
          your eyes.

Pause.

VERA. I love you. I just want to say that. I don't mean anything by it. Lance loves you too, I know he does. That's one more reason why I couldn't possibly, so it's all right to say it. You won't feel it's an overture. People feel being loved is a pressure, they like it better if you don't care, I used to notice that in the days when I felt I had to and one of the reasons I didn't take to it was I always did care when I shouldn't have. But this is quite different. Lance and I both love you. And Jaq too, we love Jaq. But somehow we particularly . . . I just wanted to get that out of the way.

PHIL. I need you.

VERA. We would do anything for you. I would die. Do I speak in clichés? I *would* die.

7. Body

The flat.
Body on the floor under a blanket. LANCE, VERA, PHIL, JAQ.

LANCE. This is ridiculous.

PHIL. He shouldn't have come in here.

JAQ. You shouldn't have let him in.

PHIL. You shouldn't have / asked him here.

JAQ. I didn't, he said he had to see me, I told him you wouldn't / let him in.

PHIL. That was asking.

JAQ. I thought you wouldn't let him in.

LANCE. This is unbelievable.

PHIL.   It was self-defence.

JAQ.   I didn't know you had a gun. / Where did you get it?

PHIL.   He barges in here. Of course you knew I had a gun. Who are you planning to lie to?

LANCE.   We must get the police.

PHIL.   Are we planning to lie to the police?

LANCE.   This is just so . . .

JAQ.   It wasn't self-defence.

PHIL.   There are witnesses that it was self-defence.

LANCE.   What do you get for murder in this country?

Pause.

VERA.   Maybe he isn't dead.

Pause.

LANCE.   I don't like the idea of committing perjury. I don't think I'd be very good at it. And Vera's extremely truthful, she gets a funny look round the mouth if she's even just modifying the truth.

JAQ.   You'll need a good lawyer.

LANCE.   No, we're witnesses not – no, yes, I guess you're, yes, we could be held as accessories, the whole thing could snowball and would they keep us in the country till they – I have to be back home by Labour Day.

PHIL.   But you've got to say, you've got to / help, you –

LANCE.   I came here for a vacation.

Pause.

LANCE.   You going to prison isn't going to bring him back.

Pause.

PHIL.   I think we should just dump him in Epping
           Forest.

LANCE.   Where's that?

JAQ.   Not far. It's nice. It's a nice forest.

8.   Breakfast

LANCE *and* VERA *at breakfast in hotel.*

LANCE.   I can't eat this.

VERA.   It's an English breakfast.

LANCE.   I can't eat it.

VERA.   We've paid for it anyway. Bed and Breakfast.
           They don't give you a discount.

LANCE.   If I've paid for it the money's gone. Start from
           there. Do I want this greasy muck? / No. I

VERA.   Hush.

LANCE.   would pay double not to have to eat it.

VERA.   I think it's delicious. It's only the egg is kind
           of greasy, they fried it too fast, that's why it
           has those little bobbles / where the fat's burst –

LANCE.   You eat it. You eat it.

VERA.   I can't eat two breakfasts.

LANCE.   I can't eat any breakfast.

VERA.   You'll be hungry at lunch.

           Pause.

           It's not economic.

           Pause.

           It looks suspicious. We have to act natural.

People will remember you didn't . . .

Pause.

Give me your mushroom. And the tomato.

He does. He picks up the newspaper and reads. She eats.
Pause.

VERA.   So what's new?

LANCE.   Things aren't getting too much farther in the middle east.

VERA.   Good.

Pause.
He puts the paper down.

VERA.   Don't cry. Don't cry.

Pause.

Do you feel ill? Do you have a temperature? Do you want to go lie down?

9. Walk

LANCE *and* VERA *in the country with a map.*

LANCE.   Do you think he's insane?

VERA.   What *is* insane?

LANCE.   If he didn't know what he was doing.

VERA.   Are *we* insane?

LANCE.   I was insane / not to call the police.

VERA.   But not *insane*. If we're not insane and he is, he'd get off / and we'd go to prison.

LANCE.   Not *off*, a mental hospital isn't my idea of off, Broadmoor / is hardly –

VERA.   I don't think he *is* insane like Broadmoor, isn't
          that mass murderers and I don't know
          werewolves or you know what I mean isn't
          that for weirdos / and I don't think he is,

LANCE.   And isn't he –

VERA.   I think he's a psychopath, / which means he

LANCE.   I think all these terms –

VERA.   knows what he's doing but he doesn't care, a
          psychopath / does mean something,

LANCE.   I don't think these terms –

VERA.   it's not like schizophrenic / which –

LANCE.   Schizophrenic does mean something.

VERA.   OK, it means *something* but there's a lot of
          debate about like is it your family or is it
          chemical and is it a positive thing / or a

LANCE.   Not nowadays, it's not positive nowadays.

VERA.   sickness or adapting to a sick environment /
          which we all have to –

LANCE.   I think this is hippy thinking.

VERA.   Well I don't think he is that, I think he's a
          psychopath / which means you can't do

LANCE.   I think he's a shit.

VERA.   anything for them, they just don't feel the
          consequences of their actions, I mean more
          than most people, we can all get *over* the
          consequences, I do think we can and should, I
          think it's our duty / to get over it.

LANCE.   It might be our duty not to.

VERA.   No, because we didn't do it, he did it, if we'd
          done it it might be different, but whatever, I
          think you have to be positive and somehow
          assimilate / the experience –

LANCE.   I think he's a shit.

VERA.   Yes, sure he's a shit, a psychopath *is* a shit.

LANCE.   He manipulated us, I wouldn't be surprised he planned the whole thing so he'd have us to help him, / he knew he could count on us

VERA.   That would be premeditated.

LANCE.   because we're his family. So it was premeditated.

VERA.   It could have been. If you're a psychopath / you –

LANCE.   If you're a shit.

VERA.   I thought he was beautiful at first. He looks like a weasel.

Pause.

LANCE.   And the girl, what about her?

VERA.   I suppose she is his sister?

LANCE.   What? Why not?

VERA.   I don't know anything about them any more.

LANCE.   Now she's a weirdo.

Pause.

VERA.   We came up here to get away from it. Why don't we look at the map?

LANCE.   Because we know where we are. We follow the footpath.

VERA.   I like to see on the map. And I'm not sure we do follow the footpath because look, we should have turned off here / down that other –

LANCE.   Where was that?

VERA.   By the field with the bull.

LANCE.   I'm not going through a field with a bull.

VERA.   They *have* bulls in English fields, they don't hurt you.

LANCE. We can get round here by this path, look, it brings us back. Shall we do that? Look. I thought you were the one who liked maps.

VERA. Ok, we'll do that.

LANCE. But look.

VERA. I don't care.

Pause.

VERA. What do you think they're saying about us?

LANCE. They're probably laughing.

VERA. No, I think they're grateful. We make them feel secure.

Pause.

We could go to the police in Chipping Camden.

LANCE. You don't go to the police about your own family.

VERA. That isn't necessarily so.

Pause.

LANCE. I think he's crazy. He has a crazy look.

VERA. Maybe it runs in the family.

LANCE. You think I look crazy?

VERA. It was a joke.

LANCE. I think I am. I think I'm crazy now. I think this has driven me crazy.

VERA. Let's walk, we don't feel so bad.

Pause.

LANCE. I think his hand moved. In the forest. I think his hand moved a leaf. If he wasn't dead then, it wasn't too late *then* when I thought it was too late, if only I'd realised, if only I'd dared, but now it really is too late.

VERA.	He was dead, it was too late then. But it's not too late now / to –
LANCE.	It is too late now.
	Pause.
VERA.	I like her, I really feel sorry for her.
LANCE.	Is *she* insane?

10. Quarrel

All four at the flat. PHIL *asleep. The others sitting about. Long silence.*

JAQ.	You could go to the zoo.
VERA.	I've seen animals.
JAQ.	But every zoo's / different.
VERA.	I don't like animals in cages. I don't like animals.
JAQ.	You've been to the Tower? You've been to Madame Tussaud's?
	Pause.
	You could go in a boat up the river.
	Pause.
VERA.	*You* could go on a boat up the river. Do you want to? No, neither do I. I'm in terror. How do I go on a boat? I can't read a magazine. I can't go five minutes without UH this horrible thing hits inside me, *that happened*, what do you do with that, go on a boat? In the country we got in a panic, that's why we came back, do you think we *wanted* to see you, we had to see you that's all, because it's less horrible, the grass was so green it was threatening, the trees you felt someone was going to jump out, you

felt the *tree* was going to jump out, and at least here we're *facing* . . .

Silence.

LANCE. When you belong somewhere you don't need to rush round seeing things all the time, you don't have to be a tourist, you're a visitor sure but you stay a while, you have family here, you can sit down and do nothing all day, it's great.

Silence.

JAQ. Nothing in the Gazette.

LANCE. What we really need is the Epping Gazette. Do they have an Epping Gazette?

Pause.
PHIL *wakes suddenly,* VERA *is startled then realises.*

PHIL. Uh.

VERA. What? Oh.

PHIL. I was dreaming, I dreamt . . . there was this . . . we were all . . . then it changed and . . . it was extraordinary because . . . and then I . . . the answer, the answer was orange. I wish you wouldn't wake me up.

JAQ. We didn't wake you up, / you just –

PHIL. I'm awake aren't I?

VERA. You woke yourself up.

PHIL. No one can sleep with all these people in the room.

LANCE. Go in the bedroom.

PHIL. Who lives here? Do you think you're at home? Why don't you get off my back? Why don't you go back to a hotel and / have a holiday?

LANCE. Because we've no money because we lent you / five hundred pounds.

PHIL.   So you think you've bought me, you can live
               in my flat, wake me up from my dream,
               typical American think you can take the place
               over, think people like you, nobody likes
               you, / you are very

LANCE.   You have killed a man. / You have killed.

JAQ.   We know that. Do you have to

PHIL.   boring, very patronising, / very insincere, very
               ugly, very selfcentred –

VERA.   It's you you're describing, it's a game where

JAQ.   tell us that? You sit about suffering, you make
               it your *problem*.

VERA.   you get people to describe / what they most

PHIL.   Why don't you go home?

LANCE.   What about our money? / We're going home
               on Friday.

PHIL.   You've plenty of money.

LANCE.   We do not have money.

VERA.   don't like and it's always what *they're* – You
               think it's not a problem?

JAQ.   You're so important.

II   US

1. Shrink

Vera *lying on couch,* SHRINK *sitting at her head.*

VERA.   I'd lost a child and I was looking for it in a chest of drawers. I was going through these drawers pulling out sweaters and I found some kittens, there were kittens everywhere but I still hadn't found the child and I hadn't been looking after the kittens so they were dying, I kept putting them in the water in the sink and all I had at the end was socks, not even a pair, just odd socks.

Pause.

Then there was a body on the floor and it was me and as I looked at it it moved, I was terrified, it meant it was about to be the end of the world.

Pause.

There's not having had a child of course is the lost child. And the child in me I've lost. Odd socks is perfect. And I do feel dead and I do feel I'm going to be judged.

Pause.

My descendants are dead because they're never going to exist and my ancestors are dead partly because everyone's ancestors are dead but because they were killed, so many of them were killed, and sometimes I can feel that and sometimes I can't. If I think of my father and

try to think of a boy of six in Russia seeing his
mother cut open from her breast to her
stomach . . . it's embarrassing, why, because
he never mentioned it, my mother said it at
his funeral and wouldn't talk about it again. I
see her naked which is wrong. She would have
been wearing . . . I give up, I turn it into a
Russian doll. And my mother was got out of
Germany so she never saw anything, but her
parents, her two sisters, her little brother, all
gone, how would you understand that if you
hadn't seen them for months anyway? She
wouldn't speak either. She wanted me to be
happy.

Pause.

There's something I'm not telling you.

Pause.

When I was in England someone was killed. I
was there in the room, I'd never seen anyone
dead. One minute he was –. And I joined in, I
helped bury him in a wood at night, we put
the dead leaves over, we ran all round in the
dead leaves so they'd all be churned up so
nobody –. And nobody ever did find him.
Didn't he have a family? Didn't someone care
if he was dead?

Pause.

I'm telling you something true, that wasn't a
dream.

SHRINK.   You feel guilt for the deaths in your family
because you are a survivor. You and your
parents buried them with silence.

VERA *sits up and faces him.*

VERA.   Go for the police. I'm a murderer.

He doesn't react. She lies down.

SHRINK.   The child is lost but your dead body is coming
back to life. You are frightened by the day of

judgment because it means living with the consequences of your actions, which you feel include these deaths. Your past self should be in a drawer where you can find it but it has split into many defenceless creatures dying of neglect. You are letting yourself die as an expiation, and similarly killing your children by not allowing them to live. The water is to drown the kittens but also to wash them clean. They turn into part of your everyday life. The man in the wood is your dead ancestors, your unborn children and the part of yourself you fear to have discovered. When you ask me to go for the police you are asking me to discover this self and help you to face the consequences. Which is what I am trying to do now.

Pause.

The man in the wood is also me.

2. **Bar**

LANCE *and a* COLLEAGUE *in a bar.*

COLL.   So sales are down, this is seasonal. The guy should know it's seasonal, he has access to the figures, or what kind of a hell job is he doing?

            Pause.

            I mean it's seasonal.

LANCE.   It is, it's the time of year.

COLL.   That's what I'm saying. But does he see that?

            Silence.

LANCE.   What's the worst thing you ever did?

COLL.   Well now, two years back, the figures really took a dip / and that was in –

LANCE.   No, I don't mean sales. I mean in your life.

COLL.   The worst? The worst thing that happened to me / was when that fire –

LANCE.   No, the worst thing you did. You did it. Not it happened. You did. Something.

COLL.   The worst thing I did.

LANCE.   Yes.

COLL.   Why what's the worst thing you did?

LANCE.   You first.

COLL.   Ok. Well I haven't told anyone this, Ok. It's about five years ago. The kids were in camp, my wife's mother was sick so she'd – you get the picture. All alone in a hot summer. So one weekend I lit out, I was I don't even know where, some small town I stopped for a soda. There's a girl in the drugstore, red hair, maybe not all that special, I don't know. We just looked at each other and hey. We didn't even say very much, just hi, that kind of stuff. We get in my car and drive off down some track she told me and we come to a river, and we take all our clothes off and first of all we swim in the river, and afterwards we throw ourselves down on the grass, soaking wet, and we do it all afternoon, and on till it gets dark, we just keep on doing it.

LANCE.   And then?

COLL.   That's it, what do you think? We picked ourselves up around midnight and I explained I had to get home and she said she did too.

LANCE.   She wanted to do it? You didn't, I mean, / if it was rape I –

COLL.   What are you saying? Didn't I tell you? / What do you think I am?

LANCE.   Ok Ok I'm sorry. And when you / left –

COLL.   For Chrissakes.

LANCE. Ok I'm sorry, Ok? And when you left her she wasn't upset?

COLL. She was in the same situation as me, her old man was out of town.

LANCE. That was the worst thing?

COLL. It sure was.

LANCE. Made you feel bad?

COLL. Made me feel real bad. I'd never cheated on Marianne before.

LANCE. Did you ever tell her?

COLL. No now hey don't you ever let on to Marianne. I thought did I ought to tell her and then I thought hell it only make her unhappy. It was all over, it wasn't somebody I was ever going to see. It was in another state. But I did feel bad for a while there. Every now and again there we'd be and it'd hit me.

LANCE. But you liked it too?

COLL. Oh sure, I liked it. I liked it a lot.

Pause.

So what's your worst thing?

Pause.

Come on, don't pull out on me. What you been up to behind Vera's back?

Pause.

You won't tell Vera what I told you. In case she might mention.

LANCE. Yes, that's it, there was a girl in England. Vera never knew anything about it. We drove out to a forest, one night. I bumped into a tree because I couldn't see. There were dead leaves all over the ground. We ran round in the leaves.

COLL. What she look like the girl?

Pause.

You don't even want to talk about it, huh, you feel that bad?

Pause.

Come on, guy, these things happen. It was in another country.

3.   Passport Control

PHIL *and* JAQ *in the (unseen) passport control queue.*
Handbaggage, passports. Now and then they shuffle forward.

JAQ.   Do you think this is the right place to be? It's such a long queue.

PHIL.   Look / over there.

JAQ.   There might be a quicker – I don't recognise any of these people. Where are the people from our plane?

PHIL.   Look.

JAQ.   What?

PHIL.   It's a policeman.

JAQ.   So?

PHIL.   It's an actual American cop with a gun. Look at that holster. We're actually in America, you realise that?

JAQ.   That's the couple with the baby, they were on our flight.

PHIL.   Did you see that?

JAQ.   What?

PHIL.   That man with the glasses – look – / he's gone

JAQ.   What?

PHIL.   back, he got shouted at because he didn't wait
            behind the line.

JAQ.   What line?

PHIL.   Look, the line. You mustn't cross the line
            while you're waiting your turn. / He got
            shouted –

JAQ.   In case you rush the passport control.

PHIL.   Yes, in case you break into America.

JAQ.   But anyway the cop would shoot / you down.

PHIL.   In a hail of bullets.

JAQ.   Look at that one, in the third / booth.

PHIL.   Which one, / the passenger?

JAQ.   The official, the passport / one.

PHIL.   Yes, what about him?

JAQ.   I don't know, he just looks American.

PHIL.   He does, he looks really American.

JAQ.   That's because we're in America.

PHIL.   We are. That's where we are.

4.   Party

LANCE, VERA, JAQ *and* FELLOW GUEST *at a party.*

GUEST.   If you're going to Arizona to see the Grand
            Canyon, you want to see Indians. You want to
            go to the caves where there's like whole cities
            in caves from hundreds of years ago – you
            ever do that?

JAQ.   No, / I never –

GUEST.   You want to do that. You should all go together. We don't see enough of this beautiful country of ours. Stuck here, this suburb, this could be anyplace, don't you think? This isn't what you came to the United States for, is it? Now is it?

JAQ.   I came to see my cousins but / I do –

GUEST.   But, exactly, but.

JAQ.   I do, it's true of course, I do / want to see far

GUEST.   Of course you do. This is dullsville.

JAQ.   more of the country, we thought we'd hire a car and just set off / and drive

GUEST.   That's right.

JAQ.   right across / out west and then

GUEST.   That's right.

JAQ.   down south.

GUEST.   That's right, you want to see the size of it, you want to experience – hey, Lance, you going with your cousin, / show her round?

LANCE.   No, unfortunately, no, I can't, / I can't take a vacation right now.

GUEST.   You ought to go. Vera, you going?

VERA.   No, I don't / think –

GUEST.   What's the matter with you people? I'll go with you, Ok? Show you a good time. You want to see Yosemite National Park.

JAQ.   I want to see everything. / I want to see New

GUEST.   That's right.

JAQ.   York and New Orleans and the Rocky Mountains and the Everglades and the Grand Canyon / and

GUEST.   And the caves, the Hopi Indians.

JAQ.   Disneyland / and Hollywood –

LANCE.   Not Disneyland, / Disneyland is sick.

VERA.   You'll be bored, / you'll be disappointed.

GUEST.   Are you a tourist or are you a traveller? / I will

JAQ.   No, I do, I do want to go to Disneyland.

GUEST.   show you adventure. No you don't, I will
          make out an itinerary –

          Interrupted by PHIL *and a* WOMAN, *both drunk,*
          their arms round each other.

DRUNK.   Phil's a killer, would you have guessed that?
          He's just been telling me how in London he
          killed some guy who broke / into his
          apartment.

GUEST.   Is this true?

PHIL.   Of course / it's true.

GUEST.   Hey, did you know this? What did you do? /

DRUNK.   He shot him.

PHIL.   I shot him.

GUEST.   Did you know this? / Just like that?

LANCE.   Yes.

PHIL.   He was a villain. He was our landlord and he
          was a villain / and he was extorting

DRUNK.   I've never met a killer before.

PHIL.   money from us / and he was a known villain.

GUEST.   So when was this? / You never told me this.*

| LANCE. | Last summer. | PHIL. | *He was a very |
| VERA. | August. | | evil man. I don't like evil. |

GUEST.   When you were there?

| VERA. | Yes we were in the apartment. | DRUNK. | I don't. I don't like evil. |

| GUEST. | You were *there*, / right *there*? | PHIL. | Exterminate. |

LANCE.   Yes, we saw it.   DRUNK. Absolutely

GUEST.   and you, did you know – you   exterminate.
          saw / this, this is amazing, so

VERA.   Yes.

GUEST.   what happened, so what did you do, / what
          did you feel?

VERA.   We buried him in   PHIL.   Blew him away.
          the forest.
                              DRUNK. Blew him away.

GUEST.   You what?

LANCE.   Yes, we / buried –

JAQ.   We buried him / in a forest.

VERA.   We dug a hole.

DRUNK.   Isn't this great?

GUEST.   And is it a secret?

PHIL.   Not any more.

GUEST.   And weren't you frightened?

JAQ.   Not / very.*

VERA.   Yes, I was, I was terrified.

GUEST.   *You're a heroine I can tell, / you're the
          heroine type.

LANCE.   I thought his hand moved, / yes I thought I

DRUNK.   Aah.

LANCE.   saw his hand move.

VERA.   And when they showed up, when you showed
          up on the doorstep / I thought

GUEST.   They just showed up without warning, these
          murderers just –

VERA.   holy shit / but –

JAQ.   You weren't very glad / to see us.

VERA.   We weren't.

LANCE.   We didn't let on, / we were polite.

PHIL.   You hated / seeing us.

VERA.   Not / *you*, we didn't hate –

DRUNK.   You saw the dead man's *hand move*?

LANCE.   But there's nothing, when they told us
          there'd been nothing / in the papers
          then we felt* such relief whahey!

JAQ.   No police, / nothing.   VERA.* Then we felt
                                   glad to see you
DRUNK.   You got away with it.   because we love you.

PHIL.   We did, / I guess we did.

GUEST.   You got away with murder. My god. Some
          adventure. Wow. Is this true? Jee-zus.

          They are all laughing and shouting.

5. Hospital

LANCE, VERA *and* JAQ *sitting on a bench.* VERA's *arm
round* JAQ.

LANCE.   Nurse. Excuse me.

          The nurse (unseen) passes without stopping. Silence.

LANCE.   So he just stepped out.

VERA.   Was he looking the wrong way?

LANCE.   If he looked the wrong way and stepped out /
          and the car –

JAQ.   I didn't see, / I said I didn't see him step out,

VERA.   She didn't see him step out.

JAQ.   I saw the car hit him.

LANCE.   And it threw him / in the air.

JAQ.   It threw him forward and sideways.

LANCE.   Sideways which was lucky / so he wasn't under the wheels.

VERA.   Though he might have been thrown under another car if there'd been one so that was lucky.

JAQ.   The driver said he just stepped out / in front

VERA.   Made out it was *his* fault.

JAQ.   of him but the car / was going too fast.

LANCE.   Had the driver been drinking?

VERA.   They've always been drinking / in most accidents.

LANCE.   We don't know that yet but we will find it out.

Pause.

JAQ.   I'm not so worried about the broken / bones, it's his head.

VERA.   Broken limbs can always be fixed, it's only if there's a head / injury.

LANCE.   We know there is / a head injury.

VERA.   Only if there's a serious / head injury.

LANCE.   Obviously, / that's what we're waiting to find out.

JAQ.   Or some internal . . .

Long silence.

LANCE.   Excuse me. Nurse.

Again the (unseen) nurse doesn't stop.
Very long silence.

6.   Car

JAQ *driving with a* HITCHER.

JAQ.   Where you heading?

HITCHER. Just fifteen miles up the road.

            Pause.

            You often pick up hitchers at night?

JAQ.   Sometimes.

HITCHER. You should be careful. A nice girl like you
            something could happen.

JAQ.   If it does.

HITCHER. That's not a good attitude.

            Pause.

            Maybe that is a good attitude. You are putting
            your trust in the Lord.

JAQ.   No, I don't believe in the Lord.

HITCHER. I'm sorry to hear that.

            Pause.

            If you're not putting your trust in Him you
            are inviting disaster. I'm not saying you
            deserve it. But there's nothing to stop it. You
            are an attractive young woman. That is an
            incitement. You shouldn't go about leading
            people into temptation. / On the last day the
            Lord will say –

JAQ.   I'm not. I'm giving you a lift. Do you want a
            lift?

HITCHER. How do you mean a lift?

JAQ.   A ride in the car.

HITCHER. I do want a ride, yes please. You certainly give a lift to my spirit. I was wondering if it had some other meaning I didn't get, some kind of invitation.

Pause.

You from out of state?

JAQ. Yes, England.

HITCHER. You give people rides in England?

JAQ. I haven't got a car.

Pause.

HITCHER. Don't misunderstand me, I am not being led into temptation because I put my trust in the Lord. Five years ago it would have been a different matter. But now I've been born again you could take all your clothes off if you want / and I wouldn't harm a hair

JAQ. I don't want.

HITCHER. of your head, no of course you don't, I wasn't meaning that.

Pause.

JAQ. I stole this car.

HITCHER. I'm sorry to hear that.

JAQ. My brother died yesterday.

HITCHER. My, I'm sorry to hear that. Did he die in the Lord?

JAQ. No.

HITCHER. You don't know what was going on in his mind. He may have repented and welcomed the Lord into his heart and not told anyone, and may now be in the bosom of Jesus.

JAQ. He was hit by a car. He never regained consciousness.

HITCHER. It may have flashed through his mind in a split second.

Pause.

In about half a mile, I'll tell you when, if you drop me there, and I'll just walk up the track.

Pause.

Do you want to come to my house and have a cup of coffee and a piece of pie with my mother?

7. **Coffee**

JAQ *having coffee with the* HITCHER *and his* MOTHER.

MOTHER. We were sitting right up on the roof. Don't ask me why, I was four years old. I don't know if they thought the world would end by flood and we'd be safe up there a bit longer, I don't think they thought it out too good. I remember I had to go to the bathroom and my ma held me out off of the roof. And it got to sunset and everybody was saying hallelujah. I don't remember us climbing back down though that's what must have happened. What I do know is the next day was my best friend's party and my mother had been going to make me a new dress out of some beautiful blue stuff, and then she'd decided not to because the party wasn't going to be till after the end of the world so she said there was no point. And the party went ahead after all, and I had my old pink dress and I was real mad at my ma.

JAQ. But you still think the world's going to end?

MOTHER.   I know for a fact it's going to end, it's just
           people have trouble working out exactly when.
           You know it's going to rain, you see the big
           clouds piling up, you don't know at what exact
           minute, maybe you take the washing in and it
           blows over. Now Hank and I have a
           disagreement about this. He thinks it's going
           to end sometime / in the next couple of years.

HITCHER.   I'm not the only person thinks that. There's
           thousands getting ready all over the country.

MOTHER.   And they don't mean *end* either because
           they're laying in supplies, like sacks of flour
           and cans of food / and guns –

HITCHER.   Because we're going to survive.

MOTHER.   Seems like sitting on the roof to me and
           hoping the flood water / won't get you.

HITCHER.   It's going to be fire not water, it's going to be
           nuclear, and the Lord will save the righteous
           but only if they have the good sense to
           prepare themself / because God is no damn
           fool.

MOTHER.   There's no sense preparing except in your
           heart, that's where you have to prepare, and
           you won't need baked beans when you have
           manna and no amount of guns are going to
           help you / get to heaven.

HITCHER.   Yes because there will be desperate people
           trying to survive / who are not meant to
           survive.

MOTHER.   Then let the Lord deal with it himself. Don't
           you agree with me? Tell him you think he's a
           silly boy wasting his money / stocking up for
           heaven.

JAQ.   I don't think getting all that food and
           weapons / is going to –

HITCHER.   So what do you think? You think I should sit
           here and wait till it happens and get
           incinerated / like any sinner?

JAQ.   I don't think the world's about to end.

HITCHER.   That just shows you don't know, / and will be
            one of the first to go which I'm sorry to hear.

MOTHER.   That's right, it's not going to end till the year
            two thousand, and then it will end in the
            proper way, with no need for cans or grenades
            because Jesus / will come and judge both

HITCHER.   The year two thousand is meaningless.

MOTHER.   the quick and the dead.

HITCHER.   Do you agree with that? No she doesn't,
            because why should it end in two thousand
            just because that's a round number some
            people made up, if we didn't count in tens it
            wouldn't sound / like an interesting year.

JAQ.   If we didn't count from when Jesus / was
            born.

MOTHER.   No we have to count / from –

JAQ.   Not everyone does, there are other years, like
            Muslims or Jews can't count their years / from –

HITCHER.   You a jew? You telling me you're a jew? / You
            a Muslim?

JAQ.   No but or Hindus or Buddhists in India they
            can't think it's two thousand.

HITCHER.   They accept / what we call it, it's going to be,

MOTHER.   It isn't two thousand yet.

HITCHER.   she means going / to be –

MOTHER.   Of course it's going to be two thousand.

HITCHER.   They accept like English is the international
            language, it is the international year, everyone
            in the world / is going to know it's two

JAQ.   I'm not sure they are.

HITCHER.   thousand when it *is* two thousand only it won't
            ever *be* because that doesn't mean the world is
            going to end /then because

MOTHER.   There's no arguing with children.

HITCHER.   it's just a number, / you don't understand

MOTHER.   It's a millenial number.

HITCHER.   what I'm saying you're not living / in the modern world.

MOTHER.   You'll see, that's all.

HITCHER.   I won't see because two thousand will never come because it will happen before that. Then the years will start over, we'll count forward from there, one two / three –

MOTHER.   You'll get to around nine, which will be two thousand / and then you'll see.

HITCHER.   It will already have happened, we'll already be saved.

MOTHER.   Let's ask our guest to decide between us.

JAQ.   I don't think either of you, I don't think the world, I mean it could do just by chance, I mean by the way things are going it could happen, by a nuclear – or the way things – if we don't – I don't know much about it, about the greenhouse and the ozone, but people are beginning – so it could be – if it's not too late, but anyway no, I don't believe the world is going to end either of your ways.

Pause.

HITCHER.   I'm sorry to hear that.

MOTHER.   Don't you want to meet your brother? Don't you want him to rise up from his grave in the year two thousand? How long do you want to wait? What do you think's going to happen?

JAQ.   I don't know.

HITCHER.   Yes, if you're so smart, what do you think's going to happen?

8. View

JAQ *and* PROFESSOR *having a picnic high above a lake.*

PROF.   My wife died of cancer last year and that
             seemed to me very unjust. She didn't smoke.
             She wasn't sexually promiscuous. She didn't
             eat fatty foods. She didn't repress her
             aggressions. You think why, why me? She got
             very angry.

JAQ.   Who with?

PROF.   With God. With me. With the doctors. With
             me, for chrissake, I didn't give her cancer.
             I thought why me, just as much, why my wife?
             Why no sex, why no cheerful conversation,
             why should I be plunged into this hideous
             world of hospitals and hysterical emotion?
             Because my wife did not make what is called a
             good death. It's expected, there's a very high
             standard set nowadays of what you're
             supposed to be like if you're terminally ill and
             my wife did not measure up. She didn't
             develop spiritually and become an inspiration
             to her friends. She became a monster. She left
             her friends shitscared.

             Pause.

JAQ.   I think Americans are happier than the
             English.

PROF.   Do you have some explanation of that
             phenomenon?

JAQ.   Or if they're not they think they should be,
             they think they have a right, / while the

PROF.   It's in the constitution, pursuit of happiness.

JAQ.   English feel more comfortable if it rains every
             day / in August.

PROF.   So would this be because of the respective history of the two nations?

Pause.

JAQ.   This view, that lake down there, no one's ever heard of it, but we'd say a lake, a lake district, it's a different scale.

PROF.   So are you suggesting the psychology is geographical?

Pause.

JAQ.   I'm happy now because I feel I'm in a road movie and everyone I meet is these interesting characters.

PROF.   Do I come into that category?

JAQ.   No, you're sort of normal, as it goes.

PROF.   I guess I am. I guess professors are kind of dull in any country.

Pause.

JAQ.   So now your wife's dead do you still expect to be happy?

PROF.   I am more determined than ever to be happy. Anything I want, I consider I have a right to it now after what fate has subjected me to. I think the universe owes me one.

Pause.

JAQ.   What was your wife's name?

PROF.   Why do you ask?

JAQ.   Curiosity.

PROF.   Beth, she was called Beth. Ok? You wouldn't have liked her.

Pause.

JAQ.   So does it work, being determined to be happy?

PROF. I go for what I want and I invariably get it.

JAQ. How? such as what?

PROF. To take an example. I'm going to get what I want now.

JAQ. How do you mean?

PROF. Take off your shirt.

JAQ. Sorry?

PROF. Take off your shirt, bitch, let's see what you've got.

9. Ticket

LANCE *and* VERA *at their house with* JAQ.

VERA. A thousand dollars?

JAQ. Dollars, not even pounds, a thousand dollars / isn't a lot of money.

VERA. Why should we give you / a thousand dollars?

LANCE. Don't discuss it.

JAQ. Because I've got no money left and you / have got –

VERA. You stole our car.

JAQ. I brought it back.

VERA. In what / condition?*

LANCE. Don't discuss it. We are not giving you any money.

JAQ. *Give me a thousand dollars and I'll have it serviced.

       Pause.

JAQ. I want to go home.

LANCE.	Then get work, you don't have a green card there are places be glad to give you work less than the going – you can stand on your own two –. The hell with it, her brother died.
JAQ.	I don't like asking.
LANCE.	No, it's Ok, you're family, what the hell.
VERA.	The car if you'd only asked, / of course you
JAQ.	Yes, I'm sorry.
VERA.	could, it's not surprising we got mad, we got worried, / not a word in six weeks,
JAQ.	Yes, I'm sorry.
VERA.	you don't have to be sorry, I'm just saying.
LANCE.	Are you Ok to go home and be on your own?
VERA.	Yes, why don't you stay with us till you get *over . . ?*
JAQ.	No, because one of the people I met, he was a university professor, we were having a picnic up above a lake, and we were near the edge of where it sloped down sort of fell quite steeply down to the lake, because the view was really spectacular, and I gave him a push / because he was going to attack me,
LANCE.	Hey.
JAQ.	he was / starting to
LANCE.	What are you saying?
JAQ.	attack me, / I gave him quite a hard push and
VERA.	How do you mean, attack?
JAQ.	he / went over backwards and lost his balance
LANCE.	You pushed him over the edge? Was he hurt or what?
JAQ.	and slipped down the first part and I thought he'd get hold of a tree / but he went right over.

VERA.   My god, oh my, oh . . . That is just . . . isn't that just the most . . .

Pause.

LANCE.   Right over and what? all the way down to the lake are you saying? and what? / Did he

VERA.   So what led up to this, what exactly did he . . ?

LANCE.   drown in the lake? / Did you climb down

JAQ.   I expect . . .

LANCE.   and look? Did you / get the police?

JAQ.   So I'd better go home.

Pause.

LANCE.   What the hell are you telling us? you telling us you killed him? you killed him and drove off, you drove off, you go round killing people, you think you can go round killing, / you can

VERA.   Was it self-defence? It was self-defence.

LANCE.   just go home? / What are you saying? Did

JAQ.   I didn't know him.

LANCE.   anyone see you?

JAQ.   No, there was no one / about.

LANCE.   Did anyone get the number of the car / as you

VERA.   Oh my god.

LANCE.   drove off? / Or earlier if you stopped for gas

JAQ.   No, there wasn't anyone.

LANCE.   or you stopped for a coke, / where did you

JAQ.   No.

LANCE.   meet the guy? someone's going to be able to connect you with him, when they find him, / someone's going to know who he is.

VERA.   A professor of what?

JAQ.   I don't know, I think history, / something –

VERA.   Where was this? what university / was he a
           professor at?

LANCE.   What the hell does it matter what subject what
           university, he'll be found, / he'll be identified,

JAQ.   It's a very remote lake.

LANCE.   what do you know about remote, nothing's
           remote, did you hike a hundred miles to this
           lake? There will be fishermen, there will be
           children swimming, / he will

JAQ.   It's getting cold now, there might not be –

LANCE.   be found, he will be found, and even if it's
           next year or the year after, even if he's totally
           decomposed there will be documents, there
           will be teeth for god's sake, / even if he's a

VERA.   Yes, teeth are completely individual.

LANCE.   skeleton even if it's when we're old they'll raise
           him up out of the lake / and –

VERA.   But by then they won't remember her talking
           to him.

LANCE.   By when by when, this could be in twenty
           years or it could be next / week.

VERA.   So why don't we go to the police now, because
           we just had our car stolen, and Jaq tells them
           it was self-defence / and your brother was run

JAQ.   No, I'm not going to.

VERA.   over and you were in shock, I do think we'd
           better do that.

JAQ.   No, I'm not going to.

VERA.   And why?

LANCE.   Because of in England, she'd tell about the
           forest, / we're too implicated, we're too far, we
           can't possibly get –

VERA.   No because she'd be in worse trouble and
        that's her own country, they couldn't get us
        for that, they'd have to / extradite –

JAQ.   Why don't I just go home?

LANCE. You are some kind of monster, I opened my
        heart. Are you my family? your brother,
        you're both, I was so happy to find – You are
        nothing to do with me, I won't be involved /in
        – You sicken, inhuman, how

VERA.   It's better if she goes home before anything . . .

LANCE. can you sit, vile, you are –. Hate you hate you,
        how –?

JAQ.   Yes, you better give me the money straight
        away so I can get my ticket.

LANCE. It doesn't cost a thousand dollars / to get a
        ticket to London.

JAQ.   All right, just get the ticket, I don't care.

10. Airport

JAQ *and a* SOUTH AMERICAN WOMAN
PASSENGER *in the departure lounge.*

WOMAN. The flight is the shortest part. I arrive at night
        and sleep at the airport and at half past six I
        get on a bus. Twelve hours on the bus and I
        stay with some friends who have a bar. In the
        morning I get on the boat and it arrives in the
        afternoon. Everyone will come in the evening
        to hear how my grandfather died. We could
        only afford one person to come and see him.

JAQ.   How did he die?

WOMAN. Very well.

        Silence.

WOMAN.   I don't like airports.

JAQ.   I thought I didn't but I do. There's everything you need. Food, toilets. Books. Alcohol.

WOMAN.   Do you like flying?

JAQ.   I like seeing everything get smaller.

WOMAN.   You can have the window, I'll have the aisle.

JAQ.   We're not on the same flight.

Silence.

WOMAN.   My grandfather breathed and stopped, breathed and stopped. Then I saw there was a butterfly in the room. When it went out of the window my grandfather breathed and stopped and didn't breathe again. What do you think?

JAQ.   I think it was a coincidence.

WOMAN.   I know how to think it was a coincidence. I went to university in Chicago. But I know how else to think of it.

JAQ.   I *know* how else to think of it but I don't.

Silence.

WOMAN.   Change your flight.

JAQ.   I'm not going to the same / place. I'm going –

WOMAN.   Change your destination.

JAQ.   I don't think you can do that, swap your ticket.

WOMAN.   Have you tried?

JAQ.   It would cost more and I can't afford it.

WOMAN.   How much more?

JAQ.   Can you afford it?

WOMAN.   I don't know till you find out.

Pause.

JAQ.   I want to be at home and have a cup of tea.

WOMAN.   Go and find out. I love you already. Go and find out.